STUFF EVERY

>>><<<

BEER
SNOB

SHOULD KNOW

STUFF EVERY

>>><<<

BEER
SNOB

SHOULD KNOW

BY ELLEN GOLDSTEIN

QUIRK BOOKS

PHILADELPHIA

Copyright © 2018 by Quirk Productions, Inc.

Library of Congress Cataloging in Publication Number: 2017941579

ISBN: 978-1-59474-983-4

Printed in China

Cover Design by Andie Reid
Typeset in Goudy and Akzidenz-Grotesk

Production management by John J. McGurk

Quirk Books
215 Church Street
Philadelphia, PA 19106
quirkbooks.com

10 9 8 7 6 5 4 3

>>><<<

IN MEMORY OF MY MOTHER,

CAROL H. GOLDSTEIN,

WHO TAUGHT ME TO POUR

BEER INTO A GLASS

>>><<<

Introduction

In 1965 a man walked into a bar only to find that his favorite beer was about to go out of production. A month later, that man—Fritz Maytag, heir to the appliance fortune—bought a controlling share in the Anchor Steam brewery, one of the last small breweries in the United States. Maytag ran Anchor Steam successfully for forty-five years.

The mid-twentieth century was a dismal time for beer snobs, with generic big breweries dominating the landscape. The revival of Anchor Steam was the beginning of the revival of craft beer—defined as innovative brews produced by small brewers—in the United States. People became more interested in local, fresh food and wanted good beer to drink with it.

Craft beer took off in the 1990s both in the United States and around the world, and today there are more than 4,000 brewers in the United States. With the rise of craft beer came the rise of the beer snob. In the past few decades, beer drinkers have become increasingly knowledgeable consumers, collecting, brewing their own, and reading and writing reviews. But beer snobbery is a mark of pride, not superiority. It's not about keeping others out, it's about inviting them in for a pint. From German beer halls to the pubs of Great Britain, beer has always been a beverage to share. (In South Africa, a traditionally brewed beer called *umqombothi* is drunk out of a communal bowl that is passed around when company comes.)

So whether you're having a cold one on the porch, in a pub, in your living room, or at your best friend's house, this little book will help you live your beer snob life to the fullest. Because, in the end, beer is delicious to drink, rewarding to analyze, and a good excuse to hang out with the people you love.

Am I a Beer Snob?

Before we go any further, determine whether you are, in fact, a beer snob. Check all statements that apply.

- ☐ I have strong opinions about beer and don't hesitate to make them known. Occasionally at length.
- ☐ My friends look to me for beer recommendations.
- ☐ I can spot a good (or bad) pour from across the bar.
- ☐ I can't remember the last time I had a generic lite beer. (Okay, maybe it was at my cousin's BBQ, but only because there was nothing else to drink!)
- ☐ I have been on more than one brewery tour.
- ☐ I plan vacations around brewery tours.
- ☐ I own more than one kind of beer glass.
- ☐ I own five or more kinds of beer glasses and have rules about what goes in them.
- ☐ My friends/spouse refuse to go into a well-stocked store with me because it will take me hours to examine the different kinds of beer.

☐ I bought this book.

☐ Someone bought this book for me.

☐ I'm drinking a beer right now.

If you checked three or fewer, you're a beer snob in training. But with interest and dedication (and a new set of glassware), you'll become a full-blown beer snob, one pint (or 14-ounce pour) at a time. This book is for you.

If you answered yes to four or more, you are definitely a full-fledged beer snob—but then, you probably knew that already. This book is definitely for you.

BEER

>>><<<

BASICS

What Is Beer?

Sure, you *know* what beer is—but do you know what it's made of? Merriam-Webster defines our beloved brew as "an alcoholic beverage usually made from malted cereal grain (such as barley), flavored with hops, and brewed by slow fermentation." The etymology goes way back, as early as before the twelfth century, and likely is derived from the Germanic *brewwan*, meaning "to brew." All beer consists of at least four ingredients:

water

grain

hops

yeast

But, as you'll learn in this chapter—and as you no doubt already know from experience—the results of that basic combination can look, smell, and taste drastically different. Think of a crisp, golden, refreshing hefeweizen versus a rich, sweet, smoky, inky-black porter. Variables such as the types and combinations of grains used, when during the brewing process the hops are added, additional flavorings, and even the vessels used during brewing can influence the final beverage that makes it to your glass.

Types of Beer

The beautiful thing about beer that it is a simple beverage—delicious, refreshing, and crowd-pleasing. Still, there are many, many types to know (and try!), so before launching into the delicious details, here's a rundown of some of the basic styles you'll see in the following sections.

ALE

One of the two main types of beer, ales are the oldest style of beer, made with top-fermenting yeasts. They have more yeast flavor than lagers and a more complex overall profile. For more on ale, see page 39. Styles of ale include the following:

- **Stout:** A type of ale made with roasted barley, which gives it a rich, dark color.

- **Porter:** Similar to a stout, but made with unroasted barley.

- **Pale ale:** An ale that, in contrast to a porter or stout, has a lighter, golden, or coppery color.

- **Wheat beer:** Light-colored ale made with at least 50 percent wheat malt.

LAGER

The other main type of beer, brewed with bottom-fermenting yeasts, lagers mostly have a crisp, clean, mild flavor, though the different varieties will vary. For more on lagers, see page 43. Types of lager include:

- **Pilsner:** A pale lager with more hops than traditional lagers.
- **Bock:** A darker-colored lager with a heavier malt flavor.

Highlights from Beer History

The history of beer is the history of civilization itself. Here are some significant benchmarks in the development of humanity's favorite drink.

Prehistory: Archaeological evidence of mead (a beverage made from fermented honey) and beer has been found on drinking vessels and in pictures from China (9000 BCE), Latin America (5000 BCE), the Middle East (3400 BCE), and Egypt (3100 BCE).

1800 BCE: The first surviving recipe for beer was written in a hymn to Ninkasi, the Sumerian goddess of beer.

Middle Ages: Before 1000 CE, European beer was brewed without hops. Gruit, a mix of herbs such as bog myrtle, yarrow, rosemary, heather, juniper, ginger, and caraway, gave this beer flavor and acted as a preservative.

16th century: Standardization of beer began. On April 23, 1516, Duke Wilhelm IV of Bavaria issued the beer purity law known as the *Reinheitsgebot*, which mandated that beer be made solely with barley, hops, and water.

17th century: The bottling of beer began in England, at least among the wealthy. Everyone else drank (and many preferred, and still prefer) ale from the cask.

18th century: Hodgson's London brewery began to sell its pale ale to captains en route to India, which some credit as the birth of the IPA. Around the same time, steam engines were first used to power the grist-mills and pumps in London breweries, making it possible to process far more grain than ever before and heralding the beginning of industrial-scale brewing.

1840s: The first lager was made. Bavarian brewers discovered that the beer they made in the fall and winter and stored in caves packed with ice would continue to ferment under these cool conditions. (*Lagern* is German for "to store.")

1852: European immigrants Eberhard Anheuser and Adolphus Busch opened a brewery in St. Louis, Missouri.

1880s: Mechanical refrigeration allowed breweries to brew beer year-round without risk of spoilage.

20th century: The development of the aluminum can, home refrigeration, and the interstate highway system all allowed Big Bru to flourish. Women began drinking more beer once it was available in cans and bottles, making it consumable in the home.

1915: There were almost 3,000 breweries in the United States, often in areas where German, Austrian, and Czech immigrants had settled. But five years later, Prohibition destroyed small operations that were unable to diversify.

1976: The first American microbrewery, New Albion Brewery, opened in Sonoma, California.

1979: President Jimmy Carter lifted the Prohibition-era ban on home brewing, to the delight of self-starting beer snobs nationwide.

21st century: Beer is the most popular alcoholic beverage among Americans. Although the overall beer market slowed by 0.2 percent in 2016, the craft beer market grew by 12 percent. Safe to say, it's a great time in history to be a beer snob.

Terms Every Beer Snob Should Know

Adjunct: Unmalted grain or other ingredients such as rice, honey, or syrup added to the mash (see page 25) for texture, sweetness, and/or flavor.

Attenuation: The difference between original and final gravity (see page 30), which indicates how much of the sugar has been consumed by the yeast.

Barrel: A measurement equal to 31 gallons of beer; can also to refer to a wooden vessel that brewers use to condition beer (known as barrel aging).

Big Bru: Used in this book to refer to international beer conglomerates (without naming names).

Body: The thickness, texture, and mouthfeel (see pages 73–74) of a beer.

Brewpub: A restaurant and brewery where most of the beer is brewed to be served on-site.

Cask: A barrel-shaped vessel that holds beer.

Clarity: An assessment of the particle suspension in beer, ranging from no particles (*clear*) to lots of particles (*hazy*); suspended solids can come from yeast and other by-products.

Collar: A head of foam.

Craft brewery: An umbrella term for brewing operations defined by the U.S. Brewers Association as "small, independent and traditional." It may refer to any of the following subcategories:

- **Microbrewery:** sells fewer than 15,000 barrels a year, mostly off-site
- **Small brewery:** sells up to 6 million barrels a year
- **Independent brewery:** one where Big Bru represents less than 25 percent of its ownership interest
- **Nanobrewery:** a very small microbrewery; may produce as few as 3 barrels at a time

Diacetyl: A by-product of fermentation, like esters and phenols (see page 39). Depending on the amount present and the beer style, it can give beer a buttery popcorn, butterscotch, or caramel flavor and is texturally oily or slick on the palate.

Draught: The British spelling of draft (pronounced the same way).

Ethanol: C_2H_6O, aka "drinking alcohol," the type of alcohol produced by fermentation.

Filtered beer: Beer that passed through porous material in order to remove yeast and other solids left over from fermentation.

Green beer: Beer that has not sat long enough after fermentation and/or a Saint Patrick's day abomination.

Growler: A half-gallon glass jug used to carry fresh beer home from a brewery or brewpub.

Keg: A half barrel of beer; the vessel that most draft beer in bars comes from.

Lace/Belgian lace: The leavings of foam on the side of an empty glass, indicating a clean glass.

Lovibond: A unit of measurement for color in beer (see also SRM, page 31), measured by placing beer in a device called a Tintometer and matching the hue to a series of tinted glass disks.

Malt liquor: Don't go there.

Maltose: The most common fermentable sugar in beer.

Oasthouse: A facility where hops are dried and baled.

Racking: Part of the brewing process in which beer is transfered either to a new vessel or (more often) into its final packaging.

Snob: A person with educated tastes who seeks to share their delight in the object of their snobbery rather than to judge others. (Judgy beer snobs are *beer boors*.)

Unfiltered beer: Beer that retains yeast sediments; may be cloudy; is often but not always bottle conditioned.

Zythophile: A fancy name for a beer snob.

Brewing 101

Prehistoric humans brewed beer with no formal
training (that we know of), producing a flat and
unhopped beverage. These days, modern brewing
masters put their PhDs in chemistry, microbiology,
and food science into practice with a multistep process that consistently produces top-quality beers.

MALTING

Beer starts with grain. Most modern beers are made
with barley, with a few exceptions: German and Belgian wheat beers, African sorghum or millet beers,
Chinese and Japanese rice beers, and corn beers
from the Americas.

The grain is soaked in hot water until it begins
to germinate. Once the grain hits the germination
sweet spot, it is heated in the kiln to stop the sprout-
ing. The grain (now called *malt*) is dried and either
kilned or roasted. The length of time and temperature of the kilning or roasting process influences
the flavor and characteristics of the beer (see The
Almighty Malt, page 35).

MILLING

Now the malt needs to be broken up a little. The goal is to crack the grain to expose its starchy center but also preserve the husk, which will be used later as a filter.

MASHING

The malt is now added to hot water in a huge tank called the *mash tun*. The hot water encourages the malt's enzymes to convert its starches into sugars. A rake inside the tank continually mixes the mash to encourage enzymatic activity.

LAUTERING

Now it's time to separate the liquids from the solids. The mash is transferred to a *lauter tun*, a tank with a false bottom, to separate the grain from the sugary water (now called the *wort*). In this tank, the grain husks catch and filter sediment until the wort is clear, or, as brewers call it, bright. Water is added to rinse some of the sugars from the grain in a process called *sparging*.

The spent grain is removed from the bottom of the lauter tun and can be used as compost, animal feed, or in baking. (If you think pizza and beer is a great combination, try making the crust with spent grain!)

BOILING

Next, the wort is transferred to a huge kettle and boiled, which sterilizes the wort and concentrates the beer by causing excess water to evaporate. Bittering hops are added early in the boil to provide the essential bitter balance to the malt's sweetness, and aroma hops are added at the end of the boil to, well, provide aroma and flavor. (If they are added too early, their aromatic oils just boil away.) The mixture is then put through a whirlpool to remove hops solids or proteins, after which it is cooled in a heat exchanger.

FERMENTATION

The cooled liquid is added to the fermentation tank along with yeast, which consumes all the sugars that have been nurtured along the way and produces carbon dioxide and alcohol. (Yes, beer is yeast poop.)

Ale yeast ferments at the top of the tank and at a higher temperature than lager yeast. Lager yeast ferments at the bottom of the tank and takes anywhere from a few weeks to a few months to ferment.

CONDITIONING

Conditioning is the period during which beer sits after fermentation. The yeast settles and reabsorbs some of the less tasty by-products of fermentation.

There are several different styles of conditioning. For ales, options include:

- Aging: Ale rests in a refrigerated tank for a week or so before being packaged.

- Bottle conditioning: Rather than "force carbonating" a beer by injecting it with carbon dioxide gas, this method involves adding additional yeast and priming sugar before bottling to carbonate the beer and add extra flavors. (Many Belgian beers are conditioned in the bottle.)

- Cask conditioning: This option gives the beer a gorgeous deep taste and soft texture that's rich and slightly warmer than regular beer. However, cask ale is not pasteurized and thus spoils quickly after it's opened.

Lagers are, fittingly, *lagered*, or chilled for a few weeks or months in a refrigerated tank, during which the yeast processes residual sugars and carbonates the beer. The bottom-fermenting lager yeast then settles and is filtered out.

PACKAGING

On the bottling lines, the bottles are sanitized, flushed with carbon dioxide (to remove oxygen), filled with beer, and then capped, labeled, and packaged into cases. Cans are flushed, filled with beer, and then sealed.

Kegs are not pasteurized, which is why they need to be stored cold. Bottles and cans are quickly pasteurized with a spray of hot water before they are sent off into the world.

Fun fact: Brewers often taste the beer at each stage. The master brewer at one of the Big Brus is required to take a Breathalyzer test before being allowed to leave work!

Beer by the Numbers

Making good beer is a science as well as an art. Brewers use math, chemistry, and fancy abbreviations to describe, categorize, and standardize beverage qualities such as taste and alcohol content. There's no need to whip out the calculator in order to enjoy a good pint of beer, of course, but it's useful to know the facts and figures behind your brew. Besides, sharp math skills will help you calculate a good tip—even after you've had a few.

ABV: ALCOHOL BY VOLUME

This term is pretty much what it sounds like: the percentage of a beer, by volume, that is alcohol. Most beers have an ABV between 4 percent and 6 percent. Imperials, double lagers, barley wines, and other big beers can range from 8 percent to 24 percent. ABV is calculated by subtracting the original gravity from the final gravity (see page 30) and multiplying by 131.

IBU: INTERNATIONAL BITTERNESS UNIT

Also straightforward is this measurement of a beer's bitterness: the higher the number, the more bitter the beer. One IBU equals 1 milligram of isomerized (aka heated) alpha acid in 1 liter of beer—alpha acid (from the hop cone) being the source of the bitter flavor. Most beers fall between 5 and 100 IBUs. For example, a weisse generally has 3 to 6 IBUs, a pilsner has 30 to 40, and an IPA has 50 to 70.

OG/FG: ORIGINAL GRAVITY/ FINAL GRAVITY

Original gravity refers to how much sugar is present in the wort before fermentation (see page 25) expressed as a ratio to the density of water. Final gravity is the same ratio measured after fermentation. Lower FGs indicate a crisper, drier beer, while higher FGs indicate a maltier, sweeter one. To qualify as a given style, a beer must be within a given range of OG and FG. For example, an American lager has an OG of 1.028–1.040 and an FG of 0.998–1.008; a Russian imperial stout has an OG of 1.075–1.115 and an FG of 1.018–1.030.

BU:GU: BITTERNESS RATIO

This ratio of bitterness units (BU) to gravity units (GU) is an indication of the balance between hop bitterness and malt sweetness—although balance varies from style to style. To determine the BU:GU ratio, first take the IBU, then calculate the GU, which is the fractional part of the OG multiplied by a thousand (for example, an OG of 1.060 means a GU of 0.060; multiply that by 1000 to yield 60 GU).

A ratio of 0.5 (or 30 IBU to 60 GU) represents a balanced beer, where neither the malt sweetness nor the hops bitterness dominates. A beer with a BU:GU less than 0.5 will be on the sweeter side, and one with a BU:GU greater than 0.5 will be more bitter.

SRM: STANDARD REFERENCE METHOD

A fancy way to measure a beer's color: the higher the number, the darker the beer. Technically, it refers to the amount of light that is absorbed when a 430-nanometer ray of blue light passes through 1 centimeter of beer. Your spectroscopy not up to par? Here's a rough breakdown: 2–6 is light gold to dark gold, 9–15 is pale amber to amber brown, 16–24 is light brown to ruby brown, 30 is dark brown, and 40 is black.

Hops and What They Mean to You

Hops are what make modern beer modern—that is, something medieval monks would spit out in disgust. Two main categories of hops are used in beer. *Bittering hops* are added early in the boiling stage of brewing (see page 26) to release acids, which give beer its initial bitterness. *Finishing* or *aroma hops* are added near the end of the boil and release essential oils that add aroma and flavor.

The hop plant is a bine (aka climbing vine) that grows in temperate regions between 35 and 55 degrees north and south of the equator. The plant, *Humulus lupulus*, is a member of the cannabis family, although it lacks the psychotropic side effects of its infamous cousin.

For beer snobs, the main attraction is the cone (also called the flower or strobile) of the hop plant. When they reach maturity in late August to September, the hops are harvested and the cones are stripped from the rest of the plant, then cleaned, kilned, baled, and shipped to brewers.

Fresh hop cones must be used immediately or preserved for later use within 24 hours, otherwise they will begin to rot. Beers made with fresh hops are unpredictable (that is, they can taste different from year to year, even if the same ingredients and processes are used) and come in many styles, but they tend to be delicious. Drying whole cones is the most common preservation method, but hops can also be processed into pellets, which are easier to store, or liquefied into hop extract, which is often used by home brewers to save space and time.

EUROPEAN HOPS

The traditional choice for European beer, these so-called noble hops are prized for their low alpha acid (meaning less bitterness) and their delicate herbal and floral flavors. They have been grown in Germany and the Czech Republic for centuries, are used for both ales and lagers in Belgium and Germany, and give the signature aromas to German and Czech pilsners. The varieties known as noble hops are the Czech 'Saaz' and the German 'Hallertau,' 'Tettnang,' and 'Spalt.'

ENGLISH HOPS

English hops are mostly grown in Kent, in southeast England, and impart grassy, floral, even tealike flavors. 'Golding,' 'Fuggle,' and 'Challenger' are some of the more common types. They lend their flavors to British pale ales and brown ales, and 'Challenger' is often compared to Earl Grey tea. Hard to get more British than that.

AMERICAN HOPS

American hops are bigger and bolder than noble and English hops. Their flavor may be citrusy, piney, or resiny. Some are high in alpha acids, which makes for higher IBUs. American hops are grown mostly in the Pacific Northwest, hence the geographical names of the famous "three Cs" of West Coast IPA hops: 'Cascade,' 'Centennial,' and 'Columbus.' Other notable American hops are 'Citra,' 'Willamette,' 'Simcoe,' and 'Amarillo.' (Although hops can grow in the Northeast and Midwest, the climate of the Pacific Northwest discourages downy mildew, making it ideal for growing hops.)

Hops are grown commercially in Australia, New Zealand, Brazil, and Argentina and in backyard gardens around the world.

The Almighty Malt

Plenty of people talk about hops, but the true beer snob never neglects malts, or the grains used in the brewing process (see page 24). In the United States, barley is typically used, but wheat is also popular. (Sorghum, for centuries the malted grain of choice in African beers, is used often in the U.S. to make gluten-free beer.)

To make grain into malt, it is steeped in hot water for two days to kick-start metabolic activity (basically, you're tricking the grain into thinking it's time to grow a new plant). Next, the grains are left to germinate for four days, during which time enzymes break down complex protein/carbohydrate cell walls that encapsulate the starchy center of the grain. Once the starchy inside is exposed, more enzymes are created to initiate the growth of a new sprout and to turn all of that starch into sugar. Next, the malt is dried in either a kiln or a drum roaster to stop germination (because you don't want to actually grow a new plant). The time, temperature and moisture level of the kilning or roasting step determines the enzyme potential during brewing, as well as the malt's color and flavor. Many beers are made with a mix of the malt types described below.

Fun fact: maltsters used to spread wet barley on the floor and turn it over with rakes until it germinated. (Some brewers still practice floor malting, saying that it gives beer an unmatched taste. We'll give the five-second rule an extension for that one.)

BASE MALTS

Base malts represent anywhere from 60 percent to 100 percent of a beer's grain bill. Brewers use them for the enzymes, which help create the wort and eventually produce alcohol during fermentation.

- Two of the most common base malts are pilsner and pale ale malts, used (shockingly!) to make the beers they're named for as well as many other kinds of beers. You can even find a pilsner malt in a stout.

- Vienna and Munich malts are kiln-dried at a higher initial temperature (195°F–200°F) than pilsner and pale ale, giving them a darker, stronger flavor. Vienna malts are used in Oktoberfest beers and bocks, and Munich malts make a deeper amber beer with a touch of sweetness. Märzen beers typically emphasize Munich malts, although they can be made with Vienna, pilsner, and Munich malts as well.

SPECIALTY MALTS

Specialty malts represent a relatively smaller portion of the grain bill and provide additional flavor, color, or complexity. Their moisture content before kilning (which depends on malt type and season) often determines their flavor. A low-moisture malt has a biscuity, toasted flavor, and a higher-moisture malt tends more toward sweet, toffee, and caramel notes.

- Caramel or crystal malts are kilned quickly to 140°F while the grain is still wet from germination. This creates steam while the starch from the grain is converted to sugar and basically "stews" or liquefies the sugar. The malt is then roasted at a high temperature, which dries the malt and caramelizes the sugar, creating a sweet, caramel flavor. Providing 5 percent to 40 percent of the total grain bill, these malts contribute sweetness, color, aroma complexity, and foam retention. Amber lagers, pale ales, Belgian pale ale, stouts, and porters all contain varying amounts of caramel malts.

- Chocolate or roasted malts are roasted in a drum-roaster at 425°F to 450°F for 2 hours, which gives them their roasty, rich characteristics. They make up 1 percent to 10 percent of the grain bill.

They imbue porters and stouts with coffee flavor. You can find roasted malts in brown ales, strong ales, and dark Belgian beers.

- **Black malts** are kilned at 450°F and added for color and roasty flavor. They can be found in dark lagers, barley wine, porters, and stouts. Black malts balance the sweetness of some beers, but too much can make a beer undrinkable, so they typically make up no more than 5 percent of the grain bill.

- **Smoked malts** provide a (duh) smoky flavor, which they get from a somewhat retro process. These days, most malts are kilned with indirect heat, but before the nineteenth century, malt was roasted directly over a fire—a technique some modern brewers are reviving to make smoked beer. These malts typically represent less than 20 percent of the grain bill, although German *rauchbier* can contain as much as 95 percent smoked malt.

All about Ales

Fermented with *Saccharomyces cerevisiae*, also known as brewer's yeast, ales are the oldest type of beer. They get much of their characteristically complex flavor profile from fermentation by-products called esters and phenols, which create a fruity aroma or taste. Think of the banana-like notes in a hefeweizen or the grape- or berrylike notes of a porter. (Esters can also smell like honey, rose, apples, tropical fruit, and nail polish remover.) English, German, and Belgian ales tend to have more esters than American ales because of their yeast strains.

WHITE ALES

White ales are German and Belgian beers made from wheat rather than barley, which gives them a soft palate.

- **Berliner weisse** (2.8%–3.4% ABV, 3–6 IBUs) is a German classic, cloudy and pale, with low alcohol, low hop bitterness, and a tart, fruity flavor.

- **Hefeweizen** (4.9%–5.6% ABV, 10–15 IBUs) is stronger than a weisse, with a pleasantly yeasty flavor and fruit overtones.

PALE ALES

- English pale ale (4%–5% ABV, 20–40 IBUs) demonstrates a nice balance between malt and herby English hops. It has medium gold to copper color and a clean finish.

- American pale ale (4.4%–5.5% ABV, 30–50 IBUs) gets a more citrusy and/or piney hop profile from American hops. Hop aroma and flavor is medium-high, while the malt character is low.

- India pale ale, better known as IPA (6.3%–7.6% ABV, 50–70 IBUs), is one of the most popular craft beers in the United States. It has a strong hop character and ranges from a nutty English malt to floral, citrus, and/or prominent bitterness.

MEDIUM ALES

- American red ale (4.1%–4.6% ABV, 20–28 IBUs) combines the fruitiness of an IPA with a medium malt character and low to medium hops.

- Irish red ale (4%–6% ABV, 18–28 IBUs) often has malted barley or corn adjuncts, which can lighten the body. ("Red ale" formulas vary from brewer to brewer, so expect flavors from mild to big.)

- Amber ales (4%–6% ABV, 11–18 IBUs) can range in style but typically are a malty variety of red ale, often made with crystal and Victory malts, with medium hop bitterness and low hop aroma.

- Brown ales (4.2%–6% ABV, 15–25 IBUs) are a classic English beer, with a medium body and restrained character. They can be dry or sweet but have plenty of malt and nutty, caramel, and/or toffee flavor.

- American brown ales (4.2%–6.3% ABV, 25–45 IBUs), like many stateside beer styles, are hoppier than their British counterparts. However, these ales contain the roast malt character with hints of caramel and chocolate from the malts. They have a full body with a low to medium hop aroma and medium to high hop bitterness.

DARK ALES

Porters are well-balanced dark beers with low aromatic hops, medium to dark malts, hints of coffee or chocolate, and a dry finish.

- English porters range from 4.4% to 6% ABV and have 20–30 IBUs.

- **American porters** are often imperial (see What Does Imperial Mean? on page 48) with 7%–10% ABV and 35–50 IBUs, but they can also be in the robust style with a more bitter and malty character, with 5.1%–6.6% ABV and 25–40 IBUs.

Stout has low hop perception in aroma but high hop bitterness, with a characteristic dry-roasted finish and chocolate or coffee overtones.

- **Dry stouts** (4.2%–5.3% ABV, 30–40 IBUs) are dark-colored, light-tasting beers, such as Guinness.

- **Milk stouts** (3.2%–6.3% ABV, 15–25 IBUs) are brewed with lactose sugar, which adds a lightly sweet flavor and creamy texture.

- **Oatmeal stout** (3.8%–6.1% ABV, 20–40 IBUs) gets its rich flavor and silky palate from the addition of oats to the mash. (It was once prescribed as a fortifying drink for the weak—not a bad Rx!)

All about Lagers and Hybrid Beers

The beer novice might consider lager a pale, tasteless beer that is sold by the case to people more interested in getting drunk than savoring a beverage. But a beer snob would never confuse generic Bru with a truly excellent lager. Yes, lagers are much clearer (aka contain less sediment) than ales, and they're definitely popular (95 percent of the beers made worldwide are lagers). But they also come in a range of colors and, unlike most Big Brus, they are filled with flavor.

DARK LAGERS

- American amber lagers (4.5%–5.4% ABV, 18–30 IBUs) are copper colored, with a medium hop character and a caramel malt flavor. Their relative complexity makes them a great lager for ale enthusiasts.

- Bock (6%–7% ABV, 20–30 IBUs) is a creamy, malty lager with little to no hop character and a dark brown color. (Fun fact: *Bock* means "goat" in German and likely comes from a mistranslation of Eisenbeck, the bock's city of origin.)

- Dopplebock (6%–7.9% ABV, 17–27 IBUs), bock's stronger cousin, has a lighter malt taste but strong, toasty flavors.

- Märzen/Oktoberfest (5.1%–6% ABV, 18–25 IBUs) is a classic German brown beer. Brewed with European noble hops, it gets its characteristic toasty flavors from Vienna malts.

- Black lager, also known as schwarzbier (3.8%–4.9% ABV, 22–30 IBUs), is a beer of contrasts: although it has a deep, dark color, its roasted flavor is surprisingly light.

PALE LAGERS

- American lager (4.1%–5.1% ABV, 5–15 IBUs) is indeed the purview of Big Bru, but that doesn't mean you should skip it. When done right, American lager is light bodied, not hoppy, and neutral but crisp, clean, drinkable, and well carbonated. It is best served extra cold.

- German pilsners (4.6%–5.3% ABV, 25–40 IBUs) have a stronger hop aroma and bitterness that's balanced by malt.

- Czech pilsners (4.1%–5.1% ABV, 30–45 IBUs) are dark in color and have a sweet and biscuit-like malt aroma. Like their American cousins, well-crafted German or Czech pilsners have a refreshing, subtle, flavorful character that's a far cry from tasteless Big Bru.

HYBRID BEERS

These beers are fermented with lager yeast but brewed in the style of ales—or vice versa. (You didn't think being a beer snob was simple, did you?)

- California common (4.6%–5.7% ABV, 35–45 IBUs) is brewed with lager yeast but fermented at warmer temperatures more appropriate for ale. Native to California, as the name suggests, it's also known as Steam Beer, Fritz Maytag's favorite beer, and has been trademarked in the U.S. by Anchor Brewing. A medium-to-light amber color, California common has a dry palate, malt sweetness, and medium hop bitterness.

- Altbier (4.6%–5.6% ABV, 25–52 IBUs) is a brown German ale that is often lagered. A well-balanced beer, it gets its hops from biscuity malts, medium hop, and fruity esters.

- Kölsch (4.8%–5.3% ABV, 18–28 IBUs) is a pale German ale that is also lagered. It has a delicate hop flavor and a vinous finish.

- **American cream ale** (4.3%–5.7% ABV, 10–22 IBUs) is one of the few beer styles native to the United States. First brewed in the Northeast and Mid-Atlantic, it is fermented with either ale or lager yeast and then lagered. It is clear and light in color (*cream* refers to the hue of the foam rather than the presence of dairy products).

All about Big Beers

The term *big beer* is often used to refer to a beer with an ABV above about 8 percent and/or extra hops or flavor. Because of their higher alcohol content and the resulting "warming" effect, they are often released as winter beers. (Obligatory cautionary note: Alcohol does not actually make a person warmer. Never get so drunk that wearing sandals in the cold or napping in a snow bank seems like a good idea.) If you're looking to chase away the chill (indoors!), it's hard to resist these heavy brews.

- Baltic porters (7.9%–9.3% ABV, 35–40 IBUs) were originally porters brewed in London using lager yeast and dark malts. Their high ABV acted as a preservative when they traveled through the Baltics (great surprise) to be drunk elsewhere. Flavorwise, they're rich, malty, and sweet.

- Imperial porters (7%–12% ABV, 35–50 IBUs)— originally brewed for Catherine the Great— contained extra alcohol to help preserve them during the passage from London to Russia. They're very dark brown or black, with a low to medium hop bitterness and a slight fruity ester taste.

WHAT DOES IMPERIAL MEAN?

In the nineteenth century, the word *imperial* in a beer's name added royal cachet, but in modern American brewing lingo, this term signifies a style that's big or intense in terms of flavor, ABV, and/or bitterness. American craft brewers have experimented with making not just imperial porters but also imperial stouts, imperial red ales, and imperial lagers.

- Scottish ale (6.6%–8.5% ABV, 25–35 IBUs) is traditionally a stronger ale with an intense malty flavor that sometimes goes by the adorable moniker "wee heavy." Scottish ales brewed in the United States often contain malt smoked with peat as a nod to Scotland's other famous alcohol, although ales in the days of Scotland's ancient Picts were brewed with heather instead of hops.

- Strong ale (6.3%–9.1% ABV, 30–65 IBUs) is a broad category whose name comes from its high ABV. Traditionally a winter brew in the UK, strong ales range in color from amber to brown and have a toasty, sweet, raisiny flavor. These age well, and aging can mellow out the harsher alcohol flavor.

- **Barley wine** (8%–12% ABV, 60–100 IBUs) balances its high ABV with sweet crystal malts and medium to high hops, producing an overall flavor that's rich and fruity. Barley wine is one of the beer styles that can be cellared (see page 76). Like a strong ale or wine, it often tastes better with age.

All about Session Beers

Feel like enjoying three rounds without going three sheets to the wind? A *session beer* is just the ticket. These have relatively low ABV and IBUs but still deliver on flavor. The name is a callback to the days of beer rationing during World War I and refers to the limited hours during the day that a person could have a drink—the idea being that this style of beer was low octane enough for a Brit to enjoy during said session and still be able to go back to work afterward.

Session beers are growing more popular as a refreshing alternative to today's strong beers. Session brewers have dialed back on the hops and alcohol content, making these brews great for a casual afternoon quaff or, say, a work lunch with your boss when you need to keep your wits about you.

Session beers are also highly "drinkable," meaning they go down easily, with few rough edges. They're a great choice when stocking the bar for a crowd or party.

(Fun fact: The term *small beer* once referred to a weak beer, probably 1%–3% ABV, that adults and children drank daily instead of water. Wastewater treatment plants had yet to be invented, and alcohol killed bacteria and parasites in water, making it potable.)

Session beers can be of any almost style; low-alcohol IPAs, saisons, pale ales, weisses, lagers, pilsners, and blond ales can all fall under the session umbrella. When buying, look for "day" or "session" in the beer name and a low ABV.

Although some beer snobs might quibble with the range, many agree that a session beer is 3%–5.5% ABV and up to about 40 IBUs. And if you're looking for a great day to crack one open, April 7 is Session Beer Day. Heck, have two—that's the whole point!

All about Belgian Beers

In 2016, UNESCO officially declared Belgian beer an invaluable part of human cultural heritage (along with Portuguese black pottery and Azerbaijani flatbread). In other words, Belgian beer is a certified beneficial contribution to global society—and you'd be hard-pressed to find a beer snob who disagrees.

The Belgians (and before them, the Gauls) have brewed beer since around 2800 BCE. In the early Middle Ages, monasteries were an important part of the social structure of what would become Belgium, and monks brewed beer both for their own tables and for the general population. (It wasn't just a boys' club, either: Abbess Hildegard von Bingen was said to enjoy oat beer with other nuns.) Through the years, everything from wars to bad harvests to taxes have tried to stymie the Belgian brewing tradition, but it keeps coming back (for the good of humanity, clearly).

So what makes Belgian beers unlike other beers?

- The ingredients: Coriander, orange peel, licorice, anise, pepper, cherry, raspberry, chocolate, mustard, coffee, and even certain kinds of lichen are used in sometimes highly guarded secret combinations to add complex flavors.

- **The yeasts:** Belgians were traditionally brewed with wild yeast, and other microorganisms from the air and in the aging barrels impart a unique environmental flavor that beer expert and brewer Garrett Oliver calls a "terroir of fermentation"—a characteristic so important to one Belgian brewer that, upon moving to a new facility, he cut out an entire wall from the original brewery so that he could still use the naturally occurring yeast even in the new location. These days, Belgian yeasts (no longer wild) are passed down from brewer to brewer, as beer yeast can be reused in subsequent beer batches, and certain breweries are known for their special yeast strains.

- **The temperature:** Belgian beer is fermented at a high temperature, which brings out its fruity and spicy phenols, and usually with malts rather than hops to add aroma.

- **Bottle conditioning:** A bit of yeast and dark sugar are added just before bottling, adding carbonation.

TYPES OF BELGIANS

- Belgian blond or Belgian pale ale (6.3%–7.9% ABV, 15–30 IBUs): A cousin to the British pale

ale, this is well-balanced with a hint of spice, low bitterness, and a crisp finish.

- Dubbel (6.3%–7.6% ABV, 20–35 IBUs): Medium to dark brown, has a soft malt character balanced with a fruity spiciness and low hop bitterness.

- Tripel (7%–10% ABV, 20–45 IBUs): A light-colored spicy beer known for its flavor of honey and clean crisp malt.

- Quadrupel (9%–14% ABV, 25–50 IBUs): An even higher ABV, dark sweetness, and medium hops. Its typically deep, rich color matches its formidable flavor profile.

- Singel: This style is still made in some Belgian monasteries for in-abbey drinking, so it is hard to find outside cloister walls. Although its rarity makes facts and figures hard to come by, it is weaker than a dubbel. (Note: As you may have guessed, singel, dubbel, tripel, and quadruple are cognates to their English counterparts: single, double, triple, and quadruple. Now you know a few words of Flemish!)

- Saison (4%–8% ABV, 20–38 IBUs): These are farmhouse ales, which means they were originally

brewed on country estates and have an appropriately rustic or unfiltered flavor. The malted wheat
gives saison a creamy texture, with a hoppy finish
and overtones of pepper and orange.

- Witbier (4.8%–5.6% ABV, 10–17 IBUs): A wheat
  beer that is pale and cloudy. It has a spicy yeast, a
  creamy balance, and a dry finish. Coriander and
  orange peel (and other additions, depending on
  the whims of the brewer) give a characteristic
  spicy flavor.

- Flanders red ale (4.8%–6.6% ABV, 5–18 IBUs):
  These sour beers are aged for 2 years in wooden
  vats, where they pick up the flavor of wild yeast.

- Sour brown (4%–8% ABV, 20–25 IBUs): *Lac-
  tobacillus* is used to impart sourness to these
  earthy-flavored beers.

- Lambic (5%–7% ABV, 0–10 IBUs): Often used
  as a base for fruit beers (see page 57), lambics
  can have a sharp acidity balanced with strong
  fruit notes (if included) and almost no hop flavor.
  They are fermented twice using wild yeast.

WHAT'S UP WITH TRAPPIST ALES?

Trappist ales are made by Belgian monks in accordance with the Rule of Saint Benedict—the standards that Catholic monks have been living under for centuries, which dictate that monasteries rely only on their own work to sustain themselves. To make a living, many Belgian monasteries brew and sell beer.

In order to be considered a Trappist beer, a beer must be made wholly by monks according to business principles in line with monastic values, and all profits should be used to fund monastery programs and outreach. There are only eleven Trappist breweries in Europe (six in Belgium, two in the Netherlands, and one each in France, Italy, and Austria) and one in the United States. Beers made in the Trappist style in secular breweries are known as *abbey beers*.

Fruit Beers:
Lambics and Beyond

Fruit beers may get a bad rap among some beer snobs, but the finest ones are the real deal—and they're good drinking besides.

Lambics, a type of Belgian sour ale made since medieval times, are prone to some of the weirder flavors in beer—such as a goaty or medicinal taste—so brewers often, though not always, add fruit to subdue some of the more aggressively sour characteristics. Cherry lambic, or *kriek*, has whole cherries added in summer, which spurs a secondary fermentation. (Belgian brewers use twigs to keep whole cherries from blocking up the kegs—and if the twigs have spider webs on them, the brewers leave them there, because spiders keep bugs away.) Other traditional lambic flavors include raspberry (*framboise*), black currant (*cassis*), and peach (*pêche*). Lambics can be conditioned for as long as a year before they are bottled. They range from 5% to 7% ABV and 0 to 10 IBUs.

Summer beers in the United States often have added fruit—or fruit flavor, in the form of syrups or sweeteners, which is way not cool. Fruit in IPAs is also popular, especially citrus (like grapefruit or tangerine), peach, apricot, and blackberry.

Good fruit beers emphasize a balance between the original brew and the fruit flavor. How to tell what's worth your while? Imagine the taste of the base beer and the fruit together (or ask the bartender for a sample). Citrus flavor can balance citrus hops; strawberries, cherries, or figs can support the big flavors in a strong ale. Descriptors like *farmhouse*, *Belgian*, *rustic*, *sour*, or *heirloom*, or any seemingly authentic French or Flemish terms (to the best of your ability to translate, anyway) usually indicate a good option.

Beer to the Max:
Extreme Beers

BeerAdvocate magazine defines extreme beer as "a beer that pushes the boundaries of brewing."

An extreme beer might be brewed with melted snow, aged in whiskey barrels, or frozen and melted until it has up to 55% ABV, as if it were a distilled spirit. Sometimes the yeast is wild or other times it is (true story) grown in the brewer's beard. These beers challenge palates, conventions, or both, and they're not for the faint of heart—they're beers for the extreme beer snob.

A number of breweries have created extreme beers using pre-hops-era ingredients like gruit, heather, or juniper. Other breweries go the opposite route and use extra hops. Dogfish Head of Delaware makes a beer with an IBU rating over 600, more than 10 times the IBU of an average IPA!

Some extreme beers take "old school" brewing literally. It takes a team of archaeologists, chemists, brewers, and ethnobotanists to brew "archaeo-beers," which are reconstructed from analysis of the dregs found on shards of ancient pottery. So-called molecular archaeologists have reconstructed beers of ancient Egypt, China, Turkey, Scotland, and Finland. (Check out the Extreme Beer Fest in Boston and Los Angeles if you want to taste one.)

Extreme brewers also try to get their beer to taste totally un-beer-like, adding flavors such as French toast, pecan pie, chocolate, lobster, coffee stout with peppermint, sour pickles, gin and tonic, or a peanut butter and jelly sandwich.

EXTREME
BEER INGREDIENTS

salt	pomegranate
pork	smoked pig parts
maple syrup	pineapple
peanut butter	cinnamon
watermelon	basil
apple	anise
honey	myrrh
lobster	chocolate
doughnuts	pumpkin
tomatoes	wasabi
chili peppers	goat brains
bull testicles	pizza
oysters	tea
squid ink	pepper
glacial melt	dill
seaweed	avocado
lime	marshmallows

Bottles Versus Cans

Hamilton versus Burr. Hatfield versus McCoy. Spy versus Spy. Bottles versus cans. The optimal method for packaging and selling beer may not be one of history's oldest (or bitterest) rivalries, but it's still a lively topic of discussion among beer snobs. Here's what you need to know about each.

BOTTLES

Glass bottles have been used to package beer commercially since at least the seventeenth century. (Prior to that, handblown glass wasn't strong enough to stand up to the pressure of the carbonation.) These days, they come in many shapes and sizes. In American, the *industry standard bottle* (ISB) is the most popular style, containing 12 U.S. fluid ounces. The *steinie*, a short bottle that typically holds between 11 and 13 U.S. fluid ounces, was introduced in the 1930s by Joseph Schlitz Brewing Company. A later variation with essentially no neck, called the *stubby*, debuted a few years later, when the glass industry was innovating to compete with the popular steel beer cans. *Large bottles*, or *bombers*, hold 22 U.S. fluid ounces; bigger yet is the *forty*, which, true to its name, holds 40 U.S. fluid ounces and is often used for cheap malt liquor. Petite bottles known as *ponies* or *nips* hold about 7 U.S. fluid ounces. Novelty shaped bottles are also sold by several brewing companies (such as Lucky Buddha). Most bottles are sealed with metal caps that may be twisted off or popped off with a bottle opener, but some specialty styles are sold with corks or flip-up stoppers.

CANS

Although a prototype beer can had been created during Prohibition, this vessel made its official market debut with brews from the Gottfried Krueger Brewing Company in 1935, and it was an instant hit with consumers. Originally, cans were sold with a flat top that had to be punctured with a trusty church key before drinking. Some early twentieth-century breweries used a "cone top" style, shaped like a funnel, but the spouted cans faded away by the 1960s, largely replaced by the "pop top" style can introduced by Iron City Beer in 1963. But pop tops created more garbage as the tabs were discarded, and so in 1975, the Falls Brewing Company unveiled the familiar style of tab we see today—the "stay tab."

SO WHICH IS BETTER?

As with many things in beer snobbery, the answer is "it depends." Each style has its upsides and downsides and may be more appropriate for a certain kind of beer (or a certain kind of beer snob!). Although bottles have traditionally been regarded as the classier vessel, many micro- and craft breweries are using cans more and more to reap the benefits of the form.

But, as a true beer snob, you should decide for yourself. Here's a rundown of the pros and cons.

BOTTLES

PROS	CONS
Able to induce bottle fermentation in traditional styles of beer (such as Belgians)	Heavier than cans
Reusable for home-brewed beer	Easier to break
Have a slight touch of class	Bigger carbon footprint
Can serve as a weapon in a bar fight if needed	More susceptible to light and oxygen, the enemies of good-tasting beer

CANS

PROS	CONS
Lighter to ship	More expensive for breweries to set up as an operation
Easier to recycle in most areas	Some are lined with an epoxy containing bisphenol-A, an endocrine-disrupting chemical
Better protection from light and skunking (see page 82)	Stigma of cans as the exclusive domain of tasteless Big Bru still looms large
More portable for picnics, hikes, etc.	Potential for a metallic taste due to inhaling scent of metal while drinking
Can be "shotgunned" (not that you would ever do that)	

DRINK

>>><<<

Know Your Beer Glasses

A novice might wonder why to bother with a glass at all when beer comes in a perfectly good bottle or can. But the true beer snob knows that each glass is crafted to enhance the best qualities of a particular style. The right vessel will balance the beer's aroma and retain its foam. And no matter the glass, the golden rule of glassware is to *keep it clean*. This will improve taste, further help with foam retention, and benefit the general health and well-being of the drinker.

Tip: To shine a glass, hold it over a bowl of hot water to let it fill with steam. Then use a dry, lint-free cloth to polish it.

Following is a rundown of the different types of glasses and their best beer matches.

SHAKER PINT

The shaker pint is the most common glass found at bars. These glasses are cheap, easy to find, and versatile, although not the best choice for more complex, high-ABV beers.

NONIC PINT

Many beer snobs prefer a nonic pint, which swells a bit near the top. This minimizes chipping when the glasses are stacked and it gives the drinker a good place to grip. Most beers under 8% ABV taste good in either style of pint.

SNIFTER

Snifters are good for beers with complex aromas and high ABV, such as strong ales, imperial ales, and barrel-aged beers. Bars often serve high-ABV beers in a snifter to regulate the amount of alcohol per serving.

PILSNER

Pilsner glasses are slender and tall, which accentuates the carbonation and bright color of the pilsner.

WEIZEN

Weizen glasses are similar to pilsner glasses, but curve more at the top, which shows off the tall, fluffy, and lingering head typical of a hefeweizen and similar beers.

TULIP

Tulip glasses complement highly carbonated, aromatic beers such as Belgians, saisons, Scottish ales, and strong IPAs by concentrating the aroma at the narrow rim and preserving the beer's head.

CHALICE/ GOBLET

A chalice or goblet is best suited to Belgian beers. The stem prevents the drinker's hand from warming the beer too quickly.

STEIN

Steins are the famous big ol' beer mugs. Because of their capacious volume, they're best for a session beer. (Why the lid? A small duchy in what is now Germany mandated that all "drinking vessels" should have lids to keep beer sanitary—i.e., free of the Black Death. Prevent the plague, drink beer in steins!)

How to Taste Beer Like a Pro

Beer snobs don't just gulp down the contents of their glass—they savor the entire experience through all their senses. Here's how to enjoy every last drop.

1. READ

First, read the label or the menu description. What are you drinking? Where is it from? What does the description mention about the style, ABV, IBU, malt, and/or hops? A systematic beer snob takes notes. Tasting worksheets are available online (see Resources, page 134), or you could keep track of your tastings in a notebook or even with a beer diary app.

2. POUR

Choose an appropriate glass (see Know Your Beer Glasses, page 68). Pour half of the beer straight toward the bottom of the glass. Let the foam rise and subside, which will help it stabilize. Then pour the rest of the beer. Yes, it's a lot of foam. Yes, it takes a while to stabilize. Yes, this step will make your beer taste better.

3. LOOK

What color is the beer? Can you see carbonation? Is it transparent (brilliant), hazy, or opaque? Is there sediment in the glass? (Likely yes, if the beer is unfiltered.) How is the foam holding up? Is it thick and fluffy or thin?

4. SWIRL AND SMELL

Swirl the beer just a little bit. This will release secondary flavors and aromas as well as determine the stability of the foam. Smell the beer. How would you describe the aroma? Can you pick out separate notes of hops or malt?

5. TASTE

To start, take only a sip! You've been waiting for this moment since you bought the beer, so don't rush it. Swish the beer around in your mouth. How is the balance between the malt and the hops? Is the beer dry, or is there residual sweetness from the malt? Do you notice a point where the taste switches from malty to bitter? What flavor does the yeast have? Can you identify other flavorings or adjuncts?

6. FEEL

What are the nonflavor aspects of the beer? What is the mouthfeel (the feeling of the beer on your tongue)—soft, drying, thick, thin? (Not sure you can identify mouthfeel? Think about comparing orange juice to pasteurized apple juice to soda. Sure, they all taste different, but even if you had no sense of taste, you could tell they were different beverages through tactile sensation alone.) Can you taste or feel the alcohol? How much carbonation do you detect? Is the beer astringent? What is the finish like?

This is a lot to accomplish in one sip, of course. Maybe you should take another. (And if you want to host a tasting party with friends, turn to page 102.)

How to Store Beer

Many beer snobs stock up in advance (or even collect beers). Here's how to protect your bottles until it's drinking time.

FIND THE RIGHT TEMPERATURE
Generally speaking, the higher the ABV, the warmer the storage temperature: very strong beers keep better at roughly room temperature (55°F–60°F), ales and stouts in slightly chillier conditions (50°F–55°F), and light and session beers at refrigerator level (about 45°F). Basements, pantries, and closets are also good storage location options, so long as they're free of heaters, air conditioners, drafts, or anything that will cause the temperature to fluctuate.

SHUN THE LIGHT
When storing beer, darkness is your friend. No need to worry about light for beers that you keep in the fridge, but if you're storing beer at room temperature, place it in a cardboard box or stash it in a dark room or area. (Tip: never buy beer that has been displayed in a window.)

STAND UP STRAIGHT

Keep bottles upright. Laying beer on its side will allow the air pocket at the top to spread the length of the bottle and hasten oxidation (not good), and if the bottle is corked, the beer may acquire an off-flavor from contact with the cork. (Don't worry about keeping the cork moist—a cork that dries out is just a bad cork.) Storing bottles upright also allows yeast to settle rather than form a not-so-good "yeast ring" on the side.

WHAT ABOUT CELLARING?

Cellaring, or aging, beer is a great way to bring out new characteristics of your curated collection. Barley wines, Belgians, Baltic porters, imperial stouts, lambics, and smoked beers are all good candidates for cellaring. Best of all, you don't need a literal cellar. You can store and age beer anywhere with a consistent cool temperature, around 40°F–45°F (not the fridge, though; it's dehumidifying) and absolutely no light. You can even try a "vertical tasting": store a beer for a year, then taste it alongside a brand-new bottle of the same variety and note the differences.

3 Ways to Cool Beer Quickly

When you run out of cold beer or forget to chill your brews before guests arrive, what do you do? Panic? Curse your luck at not living in Antarctica? No! Turn to science!

METHOD 1: FREEZER

In the average freezer, a bottle of beer needs 60 minutes to drop from room temperature to drinkably chilled. The big caveat: don't forget about it! The beer will eventually freeze (and possibly explode), and if it gets too cold, the taste may suffer. Beer slushies are not Beer Snob Approved. And beer bottle explosions are *definitely* not.

METHOD 2: ICE BUCKET

This method requires more setup than the previous option but involves less risk. Put the bottle or can in a container filled with ice cubes, water, and salt, which lowers the freezing temperature.

METHOD 3: EXTREME FREEZER

If you can't stand to wait the full 60 minutes of the freezer method, this one's for you. Wrap a damp paper towel around your beer and then put it in the freezer. As the paper towel dries, it wicks heat away from the beer, so you'll get a cold one in less time.

A Primer on Draft Beer

Sure, all you *really* need to know about a draft beer setup is that beer comes out of it, but as a true beer snob, you likely have an interest in each part of the process. Here's a piece-by-piece rundown on how beer gets from the keg to your glass.

KEGS

The sealed stainless-steel containers that hold 15.5 gallons of beer are a marvel of modern engineering that allows a California beer poured in Massachusetts to taste as good as a pint at the brewery itself. Kegs may be kept directly below the tap (in a *direct-draw system*) or in a walk-in refrigerator at some distance from the tap. A keg within 25 feet of the draft uses a *short-draw system* and does not need specialty lines to keep the beer cold. (Kegs in the United States are not pasteurized and should be stored between 34°F and 38°F.) If the kegs are more than 450 feet from the tap, additional glycol cooling (see page 80) is required. This is called a *long-draw system*.

GAS

Kegs are tapped with a coupler and a tube that extends to within $1/4$ inch of the bottom of the keg. Gas (either carbon dioxide, nitrogen, or a mix of the two) is injected into the keg, which pressurizes it, making the beer flow through the tube and into the beer dispensing system. Carbon dioxide is more common, but nitrogen, which gives beer a thick, uniform head, is often used for malty beers like porters and stouts. (Note that too much CO_2 can overcarbonate beer.) Additionally, the amount of pressure needed for a good pour varies from beer to beer. Besides pressurizing, the gas also acts as a preservative and deters oxidization.

TAP LINES

These are the tubes that carry beer from the keg to the faucet (or *tap*). Lines should be cleaned every two weeks to prevent bacteria from building up and creating unwanted flavors in a beer. A cheesy, buttery, or spoiled milk smell near the tap is (obviously) bad news, as is a sour flavor (unless, of course, it's a sour ale).

GLYCOL LINES

If a beer travels more than 25 feet from the keg to the tap, the beer lines are housed in an insulated tube filled with water and glycol, which act as a refrigerant and cool it until the liquid reaches your glass.

TOWER

The tower is where the beer lines are housed and connected to the tap. As the name suggests, a *standard tap* is the type you've probably seen in most bars. The *European faucet* has a longer, thinner spout designed to minimize head. *Nitro faucets* have an elongated vertical shape containing a restrictor plate, or sparkler, with small holes that slow the pour and agitate the beer, encouraging tight bubbles and a lovely creamy texture.

Skunking and
Other Off-Flavors

Skunking is a sad fate for beer. A beer gets skunked (or "light-struck," or, in Britain, where there are no skunks, "catty") when UV light triggers a phytochemical reaction that breaks down the iso-alpha acids in hops and transforms them into a sulfur-containing compound called 3MBT that smells like rotten eggs and skunk spray. Clear and green glass bottles are much more prone to being light-struck than brown bottles, cans, and kegs.

Unfortunately, skunking is not the only thing that can go wrong with beer. The less savory by-products of the brewing process and ingredients can contribute off-flavors, too:

- Tannins, which yield an astringent flavor, are good in red wine but bad in beer.
- Diacetyl, which gives off a buttery flavor, is good in movie-theater popcorn but bad in beer.
- Isovaleric acid is the same short-chain fatty acid given off by sweaty feet and old cheese. Yum.
- Dimethyl sulfide smells like cabbages and old vegetables.

A solvent/nail polish smell is always bad, and a wet cardboard odor is the smell of oxidized beer (beer that has gone stale after too much exposure to oxygen causes a chemical reaction).

Phenols are chemical compounds that can create undesirable flavors in beer (though some give hefeweizens and saisons their clove and pepper flavors, respectively). The not-so-good ones can impart smells reminiscent of barnyards, plastic bandages, goats, smoke, medicine, stale cheese, and gym socks.

How to avoid such gruesome fates for your brews? Unless you're cellaring (see page 76), consume beer within six months of brewing and store it properly until you crack it open (see page 75).

How to Drink Seasonally

Brewing seasonal beer is something old that has become new and trendy again. Originally, certain styles of beer were linked to harvest and climate: for example, the cherry harvest dictated when Belgians made kriek, whereas Oktoberfests were brewed in March, conditioned over the summer, and served in the fall. (In certain areas, brewing season was restricted by law to the cooler months to help reduce the risk of warm-weather contamination or bacteria.)

Today, American craft breweries have brought back seasonal beers as a way to diversify their lineups. Modern seasonal beer is brewed based on the temperature when the beer will be consumed, rather than the season in which it's brewed. You can still drink an IPA any day of the year, but in the interest of true beer snobbery, here's the lowdown on the history and traditions of seasonal beer.

SPRING BEERS

As flowers bloom and temperatures rise, this is the perfect time for fresher, brighter flavors to replace winter's heavy beers.

- **Saisons** were traditionally brewed in the winter and drunk during the summer by farm laborers in France and Belgium, in particular. Recipes varied from farm to farm and estate to estate; rustic ales or ales that are labeled "farmhouse" are saisons. Modern craft brewers often release them as spring seasonals. They tend to be dry and spicy, with rich yeast flavor and fruity esters.

- **Bocks** were associated with Lent in medieval Germany, when Catholics would fast. Beer was not off-limits and provided monks with daily nourishment. Bocks are a medium to dark brown lager with a full malty body, but a lower roasty taste. Maibocks, which are paler and hoppier than bocks or dobblebocks, were traditionally brewed in May.

- **Rye ales** are also released in spring. Rye adds a spicy taste to a pale ale and a sweetness to darker beers. It also gives beer a nice red shade.

- **Irish red ale** is offered by some breweries as a nod to Saint Patrick's Day. More common in the United States than in Ireland, it has a caramel sweetness with a dry finish courtesy of roasted malts.

SUMMER BEERS

Drinking on the porch on a long summer evening may be the most compelling reason to become a beer snob. Breweries often load up pale ales and pale lagers with fruit in summer. This is not bad (see page 57), but you have other excellent seasonal options.

- Pilsners and pale lagers, which can taste thin and cold in winter, are tart and refreshing when the days grow warmer.

- Weissbier is low in bitterness and alcohol, making it a nice summer choice. The Belgian version is called witbier and has flavors of coriander and orange. Hefeweizen, another German wheat beer, is also a good pick.

- Kölsch, which is made with ale yeast and then lagered, is perfect for when you can't choose between ale and lager. Its pear and apple overtones and crisp finish make it a tasty summer treat as well as an excellent beer for fans of white wine.

- IPA is a better summer choice for lovers of darker beer, who will just have to savor its refreshingly bitter, citrus profile until the weather grows colder.

FALL BEERS

As leaves turn and the winds pick up, and squash, pumpkins, and late apples flood the farmers market, we eat warmer, heavier food—and drink heavier beer. The fall beer palate is medium bodied, nutty, and malty, with hints of clove or nutmeg and colors that range from pale copper to a rich brown.

- Harvest ale, which is made from freshly harvested hops, is a fitting choice at this time of year. Fresh hops give beer a more rounded vibrant taste, with notes of green apple and/or citrus, than their dried counterparts. These ales have a short life span and are best drunk local and on tap, if possible.

- Pumpkin beer is a modern American favorite, but its history goes back to the eighteenth century, when colonial Americans made beer with whatever they had on hand, including apple, corn, birch twigs, and other ingredients best left to history. Today's pumpkin beer is full of spices that colonial Americans could never afford, such as cinnamon, nutmeg, coriander, ginger, and cloves.

- Märzen (pronounced MAERT-sen), or Oktoberfest, was originally brewed in March and kept cool in storage (deep in Bavarian caves, if you believe the stories), then tapped when the weather finally chilled.

- As for brews to pair with Halloween candy? **Milk stout** has a mild roasted sweetness that can only be boosted by chocolate, and the refreshing balance between hops and malt in an **extra special bitter** (ESB) pairs deliciously with candy corn.

WINTER BEERS

This season's beers are big, with strong flavors reminiscent of mulling spices, leather, and sherry. They are dark and malty with plenty of alcohol. In the seventeenth and eighteenth centuries, ales were served hot in the winter and sometimes mixed with bread, spices, apples, and/or brandy. (Fun fact: In nineteenth-century English taverns, patrons used the fireplace poker to warm their beer.)

- **Winter ale** is a catchall term for beers brewed with cloves, nutmeg, cinnamon, raspberry, chocolate, caramel, figs, and more. If the name sounds like a holiday dessert or a Christmas carol, it's probably a winter ale.

- **Strong ales** are rich and fruity and taste strongly of alcohol. They tend to be highly spiced, a holdover from the days when brewers added spices as preservatives to help beer keep through the cold months. Strong ales can be spicy, but also winey or sweet.

- **Rauchbier** is a smoked German beer. It's similar to an Oktoberfest, except that the malts are roasted over a beechwood fire. The resulting beer smells like bacon and woodsmoke—perfect for a toasty evening in.

- **Dark lagers** or **dunkels** are good winter options for fans of light beers. Brewed with Munich malts, they are low in hop bitterness. Their chocolate, biscuit, or breadlike malty aromas make them excellent companions to chocolate chip cookies and/or gelt (chocolate coins).

5 Easy (and Tasty!) Beer Cocktails

You might regard beer cocktails with suspicion. After all, being a beer snob is about mixing hops and malt, not cocktails. Yet beer drinkers worldwide have long mixed their brews with liquor, other kinds of beer, and nonalcoholic mixers. Beer cocktails are relatively simple, too—you don't need a degree in mixology to whip one up. Here are five simple recipes to try.

BLACK AND TAN

Although black and tans are frequently made using popular Irish beers, in fact they originated in England. A fresh black and tan is half a glass of a pale beer, such as a lager, pale ale, or bitter, topped with half a glass of stout. The low specific gravity, or density, of the stout allows it to float over the denser pale beer, creating a great visual effect, albeit one that's ruined as soon as you take your first sip. (You can buy premixed black and tans, but that doesn't mean you should.)

To make a black and tan: Fill a pint glass halfway with lager, pale ale, or bitter, pouring quickly to create a steady head of foam. Then hold a soup spoon over the glass, bowl facing down, and pour the stout slowly and carefully into the glass over the back of the spoon, which helps keep the layers separate. Show your friends before you drink it and ruin the look.

RADLER

The radler was invented in 1922 by a Bavarian innkeeper who was running dangerously low on beer after bicycle tourists kept stopping at his inn. In a moment of inspiration, he combined a half liter of beer with a half liter of lemon soda, called it "the cyclist's pint" (or *radlermass*), and achieved his fifteen minutes (or ninety-plus years) of fame. Today, radlers are made with weisses and lemonade.

To make a radler: Fill a pint glass halfway with a weisse. Top off with an all-natural lemon or lemon-lime soda.

SHANDY

The shandy, or shandygaff, is similar to the radler. Traditionally, it was a combination of equal parts beer and ginger beer, and although its origins are murky, one theory is that the "-gaff" in its name is a portmanteau of *ginger* and *half-and-half*. Nowadays, it means lager or mild beer combined with lemonade.

To make a ginger shandy: Fill a pint glass with one part ginger beer and two parts lager. Garnish with a lime wedge, or add a splash of rum to make it a Dark and Shandy.

MICHELADA

Micheladas (from the Spanish *mi chela helada*, or "my cold beer") are a Mexican *cerveza preparada*, or beer cocktail. They can be complicated concoctions with tomato juice or blood-orange juice or any combination of savory and sweet. This version is simple and spicy (and omits ice, because watery beer is gross).

To make a michelada: Combine 1 teaspoon of salt and 1 teaspoon of cayenne pepper on a plate. Run a lime wedge around the rim of a pint glass or mason jar, then dip the rim into the salt mixture. Squeeze the lime wedge into the rimmed glass. Add $1/2$ teaspoon each of soy sauce, Worcestershire sauce, and hot sauce. Slowly pour in your favorite lager, stir, and enjoy.

STOUT FLOAT

Like a root beer float, but with actual beer. Tasty, nostalgic, and definitely for grown-ups only. Is it a dessert or a cocktail? You might need to try it a few times to decide.

To make a stout float: Dollop a generous scoop of the best vanilla ice cream you can find into a low-ball or juice glass. Then pour your favorite stout over the ice cream until it reaches just below the rim of the glass.

LIVE YOUR

>>><<<

BEER
LIFE

How to Pair Beer with Food

When picking a beer to serve with a meal, you can take one of two approaches: match the qualities of the beer with the qualities of the food to strengthen the common flavors, or contrast them, to emphasize each flavor on its own. Here are some never-fail delicious duos.

BURGER

You can match the charred meat with a beer that has a highly roasted malt, such as a porter, or you can contrast the char with a lightly roasted, slightly sweet Vienna lager. Just make sure the beer you choose has enough flavor to stand up to the burger.

SPICY FOOD

IPAs have long been touted as the classic companion for spicy foods, but in fact they're not a soothing antidote to a scorching mouthful, since both high alcohol and carbonation exacerbate the burning. After a forkful of spicy curry, sip a cool stout, whose sweetness and low carbonation provide an excellent contrast.

VEGETARIAN ENTREES

A brown ale will match hearty and distinct vegetable flavors, as in caramelized onions, whereas a slightly sweet and spicy hefeweizen lets more delicate vegetable flavors shine through.

SALAD

Complement a salad with a peppery saison. Or contrast the flavors of raw vegetables with a fruit lambic—fruits and veggies in one meal!

PASTA

Wine is far from the only thing to serve with pasta. A kölsch is an excellent accompaniment to cream or white sauces, and a red ale balances tomato-based dishes.

FRIED FOOD

A highly carbonated beer can be an effective palate cleanser and refreshing balance to oily or fatty foods. So, yes, fried food and pilsner is a highly sophisticated choice!

DESSERT

A boozy beer, such as barley wine or strong ale, makes an excellent companion to chocolate desserts, and sweet, strong Belgian tripels pair with any kind of treat. But for dessert beer, it's hard to beat a stout, which matches well with fruit and sweets alike.

CHEESE AND CRACKERS

Hard cheeses like asiago go nicely with brown ales and saisons. Soft cheeses with light flavors do well with a witbier or lambic. If you're going bold with a blue cheese or a very sharp cheddar, match with an equally bold beer, like an IPA.

How to Pick the Perfect Beer for Any Occasion

You're invited to a party, and when you ask what to bring, your host says, "Oh, just something you like to drink." As if that narrows it down! If you need some inspiration for B-ing YOB, read on.

OFFICE PARTY

Session beers are a good pick. They appeal to picky drinkers, and you can have a few and still keep your wits about you (and not end up telling your least favorite colleague what you *really* think).

BRUNCH

Go easy here, too—no one likes a drunk at 10 a.m. Coffee stouts or porters are generally low in alcohol (avoid the imperials) and appropriately flavored for the morning. For mimosa fans, think along those lines and bring shandies, radlers, witbiers, saisons, and the like.

GAME NIGHT

IPA is always a crowd-pleaser. Are you gambling? If so, go easy on the ABV; you want to be able to afford a six-pack later in the week.

FAMILY GATHERING

Amber lager appeals to both ale and lager fans. A nice milk stout might smooth over difficulties. If your family is going through a rough patch, try your favorite imperial and keep that smile plastered on your face.

ROMANTIC PICNIC

Trying to get your crush into beer? A bomber—a 22-ounce bottle of beer, often sold as part of a limited release—is made to share and is just as romantic as a bottle of wine. Other good options are Belgian blond ale for light-beer fans or chocolate porter for those who like dark beer. (If your date's not a beer snob after that, you might want to keep looking!)

OUTDOOR POOL PARTY/BBQ

Go for something refreshing but not too intense so you can enjoy a few rounds as you hang out in the sun, like a pilsner, saison, session IPA, German helles, or American amber. Don't forget your coozy to keep your beer cool!

BYO PARTY

Bring a porter if you're not quite ready to share (since many non-snobs are unfamiliar with this style). But when you're feeling more generous, bring a seasonal, pilsner, or pale ale, which are all widely popular. Save your expensive Belgians for a more intimate dinner.

NEW YEAR'S EVE

Belgian tripels are pale, spicy, and complex, and they come in champagne bottles—a perfect way to ring in the new year!

RETIREMENT PARTY

Buy your favorite retiree a strong ale, barley wine, or imperial to cellar, as a reminder that many things get better with age.

How to Host a Tasting

The only thing better than trying new beers is trying new beers with friends. Hosting a beer tasting is a fun way to explore new styles, talk about beer, and maybe even convert your friends to the snob lifestyle. Here's how to throw a delicious party.

1. **Choose the guests.** Invite your more curious, adventurous, and/or analytical friends. If they like to cook and eat, they'll probably enjoy tasting and discussing beer in a group.

2. **Choose the beer.** Organize by style, complementary flavor profiles, country/region, season, or brewery. Consider your guests: If they are recent (or potential) beer converts, go for more accessible types, such as porters or blond/pale ales. If they are fellow beer snobs, go deep into esoteric styles and brewing techniques; compare different beers made with the same hops, malt, or yeast; or do a vertical tasting with aged beer (see What About Cellaring?, page 76). Each sample should be 3 ounces, so multiply that by the number of RSVPs to determine how many bottles you'll need.

3. **Clear your space.** Limit sensory distractions: cooking smells, perfume, scented candles, etc., can interfere with your experience of the beer. If you prepare snacks in advance, allow plenty of time for the party area to air out before guests arrive.

4. **Provide the necessary tools.** Use white-wine glasses for tasting, and keep them chilled. (And speaking of chilling, make sure you have a game plan for keeping the beer cold.) Print out score sheets (see Resources, page 135), and provide pencils for taking notes. Have plenty of water on hand and plain French bread, the palate cleanser of choice among professional beer judges. For teetotalers and designated drivers, stock up on ginger beer or other interesting sodas.

5. **Figure out the order.** Will the beer be tasted blind (a great way to get to know styles you never thought you'd go for), or will you let your guests know what they're drinking first? Will you lead everyone through the tasting, or will the tasting be a walk-around? In general, progress from lowest ABV and/or IBU to highest (simple to complex). High ABV or bitterness can ruin your palate for the beers that follow.

6. Get drinking. Pour samples (3 ounces, or $1/3$ cup) into white-wine glasses. Let your friends taste, think, and take notes. Then discuss your impressions. You can pregame by sharing professional reviews of the beers to see if the group can taste the same things as the reviewer, or you can just go with your instincts. Use the terms on the next page to help you describe and discuss each sample.

Common Beer Descriptors

Talking about how a beer tastes is a bit like learning a new language, and much of the appeal in tasting beer with friends is having the chance to share your thoughts and reactions with other enthusiasts. Use the following terms to help describe your impressions (and attain peak beer snob cred in your social circle). For even more distinctive (and, in some cases, downright silly) beer descriptors, see Beer Buzzword Bingo on page 108.

Overall impressions: accessible, artificial, balanced, big, bold, deep, delicate, harmonized, hearty, light, mellow, refined

Color and Clarity: apricot, black, bright, brilliant, caramel, chestnut, cloudy, copper, dark, dull, ginger, gold, hazy, honey, light, mahogany, medium, orange, ruby, russet, straw

Foam: creamy, dissipate, fine, fluffy, foamy, mousse-like, persistent, rocky, thin

Malt: biscuit, bread, burnt, caramel, cereal, chocolate, cloying, coffee, cracker, deep, nutty, smoked, rich, roasty, rustic, toast, toffee

Hops: bright, citrus, delicate, earthy, floral, grapefruit, grassy, juniper-like, lemony, passion fruit, perfumelike, piny, resiny, sharp, spicy, sprucelike

Yeast: banana, bready, bubblegum, clove, fruity, medicinal, peppery, rubbery, spicy, sulfur

Mouthfeel: acidic, astringent, bitter, chalky, chewy, cloying, creamy, crisp, dry, earthy, effervescent, fizzy, flat, full-bodied, grainy, harsh, hollow, honey, musty, oily, rich, silky, soft, tannic, thin, velvety, warming, watery

Flavor: aggressive, assertive, balanced, cigar, crisp, dark fruit, leather, metallic, mineraly, oaken, robust, sharp, smooth, sour, stone fruit, syrupy, tart, woody

Alcohol: boozy, complex, full, heavy, hot (too much alcohol), powerful, warming

GENERALLY CONFUSING AND/OR RIDICULOUS DESCRIPTORS

Menacing	Artichoke
Crushable	Omelet
Alien	Clay-like
Grilled	Rendered fat
Turnip	Worn clothes
Sexy	Soupy
Honeyed	

Beer Buzzword Bingo

Half the fun in reviewing beer (or reading beer reviews) is hearing all the uniquely crazy words beer snobs like to throw around. Use this scorecard of common terms for your own beer-snob-approved drinking game.

dank	coconut	tremendous	jam(my)	cakey
notes	bomb	autumnal	bandwagon	pesto
rounded	ashes	FREE SIP	watery	moody
catty	roller coaster	quaff	oily	outrageous
twangy	moreish	zippy	behemoth	epic

How to Drink Local

To quote Pliny the Elder: *cerevisia recens est bona, cerevisia localis est recens*. Okay, maybe he didn't actually say that, but it's true nonetheless: fresh beer is good beer, and local beer—since it doesn't have to travel far—tends to be fresh. There are over 4,000 craft breweries, microbreweries, and brewpubs in the United States, and most Americans have a brewery within a 10-mile radius of home. Here's how to get acquainted—if not downright friendly—with your local beer maker.

- **Support your local taproom or brewery.** Not only does this give you access to fresh beer, it also puts money into the local economy. Local breweries employ local people. They may donate their spent grain to nearby farmers. And as small-business owners, they are more likely to spend their profits at other small businesses. Last, but certainly not least, taprooms are a great place to learn about beer, develop and refine your tastes, and meet other beer snobs.

- **Know your beer distribution.** Many beers that seem to be independent—even ones brewed locally—are in fact owned by Big Bru. Research your favorite brands and stay informed. There's nothing wrong with having pride in a mass-distributed beer from your region, but going truly local gives back a lot more to your community.

- Spread the word. Make a point of patronizing bars and liquor stores that stock local beers. If your favorite bar doesn't serve brews made in your area on tap, ask them to. Introduce your friends to local beers that you think they would love, or host a tasting of local beers and discuss as a group (see page 102).

- Be an activist. If you want to take your commitment to local brews even further, join the Support Your Local Brewery Program, an activist group that encourages fair treatment for small and independent producers by addressing issues that affect brewers, such as state business regulations and revising arcane liquor laws. Find out more at brewersassociation.org.

WACKY
LIQUOR LAWS

Liquor laws can be quirky, to say the least, and they vary from state to state. License boards determine everything from whether your local brewery can sell growlers to whether grocery stores can sell beer on Sundays (or at all). Much of what is made or grown in your area is determined by local laws and limitations.

A few wacky laws:

- In Ohio it is illegal to get a fish drunk, even though no one knows how to tell if a fish is drunk.
- In North Dakota beer and pretzels cannot be sold together. (Are clichés illegal in North Dakota?)
- In Texas you can drink only three sips of beer while standing.

But not all lawmakers are uptight about beer: there is a small bipartisan brewers caucus in the House of Representatives. See if your representative is involved!

8 Uses for Stale Beer

Got a six-pack in the fridge that's way past its prime? Whether leftover beer is stale or just unwanted, here are eight ways to use it up.

1. **Marinate meat.** Beer tenderizes meat and works great in a marinade. Marinate chicken with a bottle of a lighter beer, the juice of 1 lemon, a few tablespoons of olive oil, and a couple sliced garlic cloves. Darker beers work well with red meat.

2. **Add beer to your favorite chili recipe.** Substitute beer for the broth or water called for in the recipe. The alcohol cooks off and leaves a rich, layered taste suitable for all ages.

3. **Catch garden pests.** Slugs are happy to drink stale beer—and conveniently drown themselves in the process. Pour beer into a saucer or empty cat food container and place it in your garden to attract slugs in a several-foot radius. (Unlike a beer snob, slugs won't travel far for beer, so if your garden is large, you might need a six-pack.)

4. **Bake some bread.** A dark beer gives bread in this recipe a dense, pumpernickel-like character.

> 3 cups flour
>
> 2 teaspoons baking powder
>
> 1 teaspoon salt
>
> 12 ounces stout, dunkel, or porter
>
> $1/4$ cup maple syrup
>
> 2 teaspoons ground mustard seeds
>
> 1 tablespoon whole caraway seeds

Preheat oven to 400°F. Grease a 9-by-5-inch loaf pan. In a large mixing bowl, combine all ingredients and mix thoroughly with a wooden spoon. Pour into prepared pan and bake for 50–60 minutes, or until a cake tester or toothpick inserted into the center comes out clean.

5. **Give your plants a drink.** The yeast and sugars in beer can boost plant growth, so if you have brown spots in your yard or a wilting garden, mix a bottle of beer with 1 gallon of water and water your plants with it.

6. **Supercharge your compost.** A bottle of beer and 1 cup of ammonia mixed in 4 gallons of water is a great "tea," or nutrient-rich supplement, to encourage healthy decomposition in outdoor compost.

7. **Catch indoor pests.** Got fruit flies? Pour a bit of beer into a shallow bowl, cover it with plastic wrap, and poke little holes in the plastic. Fruit flies can get in, but they can't get out. At least they'll die happy!

8. **Clean your bling.** Place gold or copper jewelry in a small beer bath. Rinse with water and polish with a microfiber cloth for extra shine. When someone compliments your jewelry, smile mysteriously.

How to Get the Most Out of Beer Festivals

The true beer snob knows that beer festivals aren't all dirndl skirts and lederhosen. These events focus on local offerings or a particular style (which, if it's German, may just involve lederhosen). After paying admission, attendees get a souvenir glass and the opportunity to sample many (many, many) kinds of beer. They can also attend competitions and presentations from local brewmasters.

Entrance fees can be hefty. Some festivals allow you to work a volunteer shift and afterward attend the festival for free. Also, festivals typically offer designated-driver tickets, which are often less expensive than standard admission and include free sodas. Some festivals put a portion of proceeds toward charities. Drink beer for a cause? Don't mind if we do.

To make the most of your festival experience, keep these tips in mind.

1. Pace yourself. You'll want to remember the beers you tried rather than have a headache the following day. Review the festival program in advance,

if possible, or as soon as you arrive, and plan your approach before starting to imbibe. Also remember to . . .

2. Eat plenty and consume one glass of water per one glass of beer so you don't get drunk.

3. Prioritize limited releases or rare brews over more widely available beers. You can drink your everyday favorite craft brew another time.

4. Try new things! It's also a great time to try converting your friends to good beers.

5. Take notes. Bring a small notebook to record the particulars of your new favorite beers so you can hunt them down post-festival.

6. Bring a designated driver. This tip goes without saying, but we're saying it anyway.

Many major cities hold annual beer festivals. For suggestions, turn to Resources, on page 134.

Will Travel for Beer: Beer Tourism

Drinking local is all well and good, but what if you want to take your beer snobbery on the road? Here are three ways to see the world of brews.

LIMITED RELEASES

How do you know when you're turning from a beer snob into a beer fanatic? When you fly halfway across the country to get a limited release from a brewery. Some breweries create a special brew but once or twice a year from a prized, unique recipe and sell only a limited number of bottles to ticketed, in-person customers. Limited releases are a great way to try beers that are, well, limited, garnering all the beer-snob bragging rights that go with it. Dates vary year to year, so confirm with the brewery website—and check early. Tickets almost always disappear lightning fast.

Highly anticipated limited releases can involve waiting in line for hours. Do be friendly and polite to your comrades in line. Do try the beer (and food, which is often offered). Do not become so drunk that you either sleep through the release or lose your hold on the precious bottle and cause it to shatter into a thousand expensive, undrinkable pieces.

For more, turn to "Limited Releases to Look Out For" in the Resources section (page 140).

BEER TRAILS

Whether you live in the United States or travel there for work or pleasure, beer trails are a great way to visit multiple breweries in a specific area. There are beer trails (also known as ale trails) in almost every U.S. state. Some trails are nothing more than a simple map marked with local breweries. Others get fancy and provide "passports" to be stamped at each stop along the route. (Pro tip: If you must purchase tickets, always ask about reduced rates for your designated driver.) Here are some popular routes.

- **Asheville Ale Trail:** The southeastern U.S. in general, and North Carolina in particular, is no slouch when it comes to craft beer. This trail offers in-town and regional walking, biking, and driving tours. Enjoy great music (for which Asheville is also famed) along with your craft brews and stunning views of the Great Smoky Mountains.

- **Beer City Ale Trail:** There are more than fifty breweries on the Grand Rapids, Michigan, ale trail. Can you survive the cold long enough to try them all?

- Gulp Coast: Who knew Florida had such a great beer scene? Starting in Saint Petersburg and ending in Clearwater, this trail is an hour's drive (not including stops) that takes you to breweries and bars from downtown to the beach. A local specialty is the Florida weisse, flavored with key lime, raspberry, mango, dragon fruit, pineapple, and/or passion fruit. You can't go wrong!

- New Mexico Ale Trail: Albuquerque has a range of breweries, brewpubs, and taprooms. There is even a trolley to take you from one to the other. Take advantage of the Breakfast Burrito Byway while you're there.

- Yakima Valley Hops and Spirits Tour: Explore breweries, hop museums, distilleries, wineries, and cideries in southern Washington state, and taste for yourself why Yakima Valley hops are some of the best in the world. One hops supplier even has a research brewery. Try beer for science!

INTERNATIONAL BEER SITES

For the jet set, here are some overseas options for beers and beer-related sightseeing you definitely can't get at home.

- **The Old Forge near Loch Nevis, Scotland:** This pub is listed in the *Guinness Book of World Records* as the most remote bar in the United Kingdom. To get there, you have to hike 18 miles over Scottish Munros (mountains more than 3,000 feet tall) or take a ferry or yacht, should you be a fancy beer snob. The scenery is great (parts of the Harry Potter movies were filmed there), and you can see seals, dolphins, red deer, and otters among the mountains and wild shores. The Old Forge brews its own beer, serves locally caught seafood, and offers traditional live music.

- **Orval Abbey in Florenville, Belgium:** Tour the grounds and chapel of a Trappist monastery. The brewery is open once a year, so plan ahead if you're dead-set on going behind the scenes. As with most Trappist monasteries, Orval's beers and cheeses are available in gift shops and cafés nearby. This is a good place to taste a singel!

- **Pilsen Historical Underground in Pilsen, Czech Republic:** Roam the tunnels below the birthplace of the pilsner (and don't forget to pack a jacket; the tunnels are kept at 42°F year-round). Visit medieval ice cellars, wells, and basements of thirteenth-century townhouses and (of course) enjoy a beer tasting.

- **Wat Pa Maha Chedi Kaew in Si Kaeo, Thailand:** In 1984 Buddhist monks fed up with litter began collecting beer bottles to build this temple, which is also known as the Temple of a Million Bottles. In a dazzling showcase of sustainable design, the walls are constructed with green and brown beer bottles embedded in cement set in alternating patterns and adorned with details such as bottle-cap mosaics.

How to Order a Beer in 15 Languages

Wherever you go, there you are. When you get there, know how to say "I would like a beer, please."

- **Afrikaans:** Ek wil graag 'n bier, asseblief.
- **Chinese:** Wǒ xiǎng yào yībēi píjiǔ.
- **Czech:** Chtěla bych pivo, prosím.
- **Dutch:** Ik wil graag een biertje, alsjeblieft.
- **French:** Je voudrais une bière, s'il vous plaît.
- **German:** Ich hätte gerne ein Bier, bitte.
- **Greek:** Tha íthela mia býra, parakaló.
- **Irish:** Ba mhaith liom beoir, le do thoil.
- **Italian:** Vorrei una birra, per favore.
- **Japanese:** Watashi wa bīru o shitaidesu.
- **Portuguese:** Eu gostaria de uma cerveja porfavor.
- **Spanish:** Me gustaría una cerveza por favor.
- **Swahili:** Napenda bia, tafadhali.
- **Welsh:** Hoffwn cwrw, os gwelwch yn dda.
- **Zulu:** Ngithanda ubhiya, sicela.

Beers of the World

Forget love: beer is the universal language. Here's the lowdown on what beer snobs are drinking overseas.

AFRICA

Europe is not the only continent with a robust brewing tradition. Sorghum and millet beers have been brewed in Africa since people settled in villages. Modern commercial African beer is dominated by a few conglomerates, which produce mostly European-style beers—lagers in particular. However, many people still brew their own beer, which is typically thick and sour with wild yeasts and has a very short shelf life. Ingredients vary from location to location, too: in southern Africa, hops are difficult to cultivate, so some brewers use rooibos (also used to make herbal tea) instead of aroma hops. Other brewers import hops from the United States. Thanks to their robust ingredients, African beers are rich with carbohydrates, proteins, fiber, vitamins, and minerals.

Chibuku, also known as shake-shake, is a traditional beer that African Big Bru produces commercially across the continent. As the name suggests, you have to shake it to combine the sediments with the liquid. It is also known as porridge beer. (Mmm, beer for breakfast has never tasted so good.)

West African *shakparo* is made with sorghum and brewed with wild yeasts found on the fermenting pots (the same way the Belgians brew with wild yeast). It's full-bodied with a sour, fruity aftertaste, and the ABV varies depending on the brewer.

Ethiopian **tella** can be made with barley or teff and gesho, a bush in the buckthorn family that provides bitterness and acts as a preservative. (Gesho is often called Ethiopian hops.) Teff is a sturdy grain used in Ethiopian cooking, notably in *injera*, the ubiquitous spongy flatbread served at many meals.

Umnqombothi (pronounced oom-kom-bo-tee) is a thick, sour South African beer made from maize and sorghum.

Utwala (pronounced cha-la) is another South African beer similar to *chibuku* and is the color of a strawberry milkshake.

Urwagwa (also known as *tonto*) is a banana beer made in East Africa and Uganda. Another banana beer is Tanzania's *mbege*, made with sprouted millet, bananas, and quinine for bittering.

ASIA

Asia is technically the cradle of beer, since ancient brewers there began making fermented grain beverages out of rice, honey, and other ingredients more than 6,000 years ago. Modern brewing in Asia, however, kicked off with the age of European colonialism in the nineteenth century, when English brewmasters set up shop in India in 1830, followed by Russian breweries in China and then Dutch breweries joining the English in India. Since then, China has become the world's leading producer of beer, and today Asia is the top beer-producing region.

Tsingtao, a well-hopped pilsner which you may recognize from American Chinese restaurants, was China's most popular beer until recently, when Snow Beer, a lager, took the biggest slice of the market. Generally, in China, pale lagers are the beer of choice, often brewed with ingredients like rice or sorghum, and sometimes using bitter melon in lieu of hops.

The *India pale ale* was invented around 1787 by Bow Brewery. Its characteristic high alcohol and hop content helped it survive the long journey from England to India.

Nowadays India's most popular brand is Kingfisher, a light lager, and other favorite brands are Haywards (lagers of varying ABV) and Kalyani Black Label (a strong beer with a sweet aftertaste). India also has a long tradition of grain-based fermented beverages, such as *handia*, a rice beer brewed for generations and used in ceremonies by the Asur tribe. (In fact, some wild elephants have developed such a taste for rice beer that they'll rampage a village in search of it!)

In Japan, *happoshu*, a beerlike beverage made with rice, corn, sorghum, and potato, and *happosei*, a non-malted alcoholic drink, are more popular than beer, thanks to a lower tax on those beverages than on *bīru*, or anything with malt content greater than 67 percent. (So-called *dai-san no bīru*, or "third category beers" made from ingredients like soybeans, do not qualify as beers and are also inexpensive.) Nevertheless, light lagers with low ABV (around 5%) from the major breweries are also popular, and *ji bīru* (local beer) and *kurafuto bia* (craft beer) are gaining popularity as well.

Singha lager is the oldest and most popular beer brand in Thailand, with Chang and Archa (both lagers) also enjoying a healthy market share.

THE CARIBBEAN

This region has a thriving beer culture, with beers varying from island to island in accordance with local tastes. Caribbean beers also have a global presence thanks to popular brands like Jamaica's Red Stripe and the Dominican Republic's Presidente—in fact, the Dominican Republic is the sixth-largest exporter of beer to the United States! Typically, each island brews its own spin on a lager, but stouts and ales are not unheard of. Although many well-known brands are owned by major American beverage companies, craft breweries are popping up more and more.

Wadadli is the national beer of Antigua, named after the original name of the island bestowed by its native people. A light golden lager, it has a sweet, malty taste with an easy finish.

The malt-heavy pale ale Hatuey Beer from Cuba has been brewed by Modelo Brewery since 1948. It enjoyed a nice boom of popularity in the mid-twentieth century—Ernest Hemingway name-checks it in *The Old Man and the Sea*, and after he won the Nobel Prize for Literature, the brewery even threw him a party. Other notable Cuban brands favored by locals include Tínima (lagers) and Bruja (pale lagers).

Balashi, a golden-colored pale lager, is the national beer of Aruba, with a clean, crisp taste and low ABV—perfect for enjoying on the beach.

Kubuli is the small island of Dominca's national beer, brewed with water from the island's Loubière Springs. A golden lager, it has a smooth finish, light color, and nicely malty taste.

Puerto Rico is home to many breweries, from the commercial to the nano (see page 21). Although the commercial breweries produce what you might expect—light lagers—smaller breweries offer more niche flavors like amber ales flavored with local tamarind, beers made with spiced yams, and even a Porter Rican, which is, you guessed it, a porter, conditioned with local cacao nibs.

LATIN AMERICA

Beerlike beverages have been brewed in Latin America for the past 7,000 years. German and Austrian immigrants brought European-style beer to the region, particularly Argentina and Mexico, in the second half of the nineteenth century. (This is why the famous Mexican Big Bru, Negro Modelo, is a Vienna lager.) Like elsewhere, conglomeration became the name of the game in the twentieth century. However, the twenty-first century has seen a rise in craft brewing (especially in Mexico, Brazil, Peru, and Argentina), and breweries from Brazil, Chile, Costa Rica, Ecuador, Mexico, Panama, the United States, and Uruguay have all had winning beers in Copa Cerveza de América (Beer Cup of the Americas). Tropical fruits, guarana, and cocoa are other flavors that find their way into South American beers, and some Brazilian brewers have experimented with aging beer in cachaça barrels.

Chicha (pronounced CHEE-chah), a fermented corn beer indigenous to South and Central America, is thought to have been a ceremonial drink among the Incans and other Andean groups. Chicha is traditionally made with maize that has been chewed and spit it out. Some modern *chicha* makers use malted maize, called *jora*; however, *chicha* can be made with many other ingredients ranging from potatoes to peanuts to cassava, all of which contribute different characteristics to the brew.

In 2015, the Beer Judge Certification Program added two Argentine beers to its guidelines: **Dorada Pampeana** (Pampas Gold) is a pale, malty blond ale brewed with Pilsen malt and 'Cascade' hops, and **IPA Argenta** (Argentine IPA), which is a bitter amber-colored IPA brewed with wheat, complete with grapefruit/tangerine flavors characteristic of Argentine hops.

AUSTRALIA AND NEW ZEALAND

The indigenous peoples of Australia and New Zealand had no alcoholic beverages before colonization. As a result, beer in this part of the world draws on European tradition and style—but with some local flavor! The first New Zealand beer was made by Captain James Cook (who brought beer with him when he arrived in 1770, thinking it'd prevent scurvy) and was brewed with molasses and leaves from the local manuka tree.

Today in New Zealand, a nation of around 4.3 million people, there are fifty breweries. The country is known for hops production, most of which is done organically thanks to few native pests and hops diseases. New Zealand hops are high in alpha acids and essential oils, and have a juicy, floral, and/or citrusy flavor and aroma.

Two famous varieties of New Zealand hops are 'Nelson Sauvin,' which imparts gooseberry, passion fruit, grapefruit, and melon characteristics, and 'Motueka,' an aromatic descended from 'Saaz' hops with a lemon/lime/tropical fruit smell. Breweries make good use of their local hops, so New Zealand is a great place to find both modern takes on British recipes and highly hopped offerings that would make a Pacific Northwest beer snob weep with happiness.

Because of the hot climate, Australians have tended to prefer lighter beers for refreshment. According to the 2016 Australian Craft Beer Survey, pale ale is the most popular beer style.

The first craft brewery in Australia opened in 1987 near Sydney, and today the craft beer culture is flourishing. The country grows hops in the island state of Tasmania and the southeastern state of Victoria, which are used in both Australian and Asian beers. (Unlike New Zealand hops, these rarely make it to the United States.) Some notable Australian hop varieties are 'Pride of Ringwood,' a clean bittering hop that imparts a classic Australian lager flavor, and 'Galaxy,' a versatile hop with passion fruit and citrus aromas.

Are You Ready to Home-Brew?

Home-brewing is a big topic, and this is a little book—too little to teach you all you need to know. Fortunately, volumes and volumes of how-to manuals out there can show you how it's done. But before you run out to buy your first kegerator, take this quiz to see if you're ready to commit. Check all statements that apply.

- ☐ I love beer.
- ☐ I have informed opinions on various kinds of malts and hops.
- ☐ I critique every beer I try.
- ☐ I often think I can do better.
- ☐ I need a new hobby.
- ☐ I have been to my local home brew store.
- ☐ I've been dropping hints about home brew kits for my birthday all year.
- ☐ I develop recipes in my head when conversation gets slow.
- ☐ I have plenty of counter space.

☐ I have space in my garage with access to running water and a hot plate.

☐ I have a warm, dark corner in my house where I could store a sealed fermenter for a couple weeks as well as bottles that are being conditioned.

☐ I have a tolerant and/or beer drinking spouse/housemate(s).

☐ I think chemistry is fun!

☐ I can follow directions.

☐ I can commit six weeks to brewing and monitoring my beer.

☐ I don't mind washing everything early and often.

☐ Sanitizing is fun!

☐ I doodled beer label designs on my notes in college chemistry class.

☐ I paid attention in college chemistry and designed beer labels on my own time.

☐ My friends love beer.

If you checked three or more, visit a home brew store near you!

Resources

PUBLICATIONS, REVIEWS, AND INDUSTRY INFO

For further reading, here are some solid sources.

All About Beer Magazine
allaboutbeer.com

BeerAdvocate
beeradvocate.com

Brewers Association
brewersassociation.org

Brewing News
brewingnews.com

CraftBeer.com

Craft Beer and Brewing Magazine
beerandbrewing.com

DRAFT magazine
draftmag.com

Rate Beer
ratebeer.com

Zymurgy magazine (subscription required)
homebrewersassociation.org/magazine/ezymurgy

TASTING SHEETS

Craftbeer.com and **Beerology** offer tasting sheets that are accessible for novices and veterans alike.
craftbeer.com/wp-content/uploads/2014/09/Tasting-Sheet.pdf
beerology.ca/wp-content/uploads/2011/09/Beerology_Tasting.pdf

True beer snobs will appreciate the specificity of the **Beer Judge Certification Program** scoresheet.
bjcp.org/docs/SCP_BeerScoreSheet.pdf

TOURISM

For the beer snob ready to take on the world.

Beer Festival Calendar
Events around the world listed by month.
beerfestivals.org

Belgium Beer Tourism
Covers breweries, beer styles, and essential travel tips specific to the country.
belgium.beertourism.com

Czech Republic
Visit in fall to catch the celebration of St. Václav in September and Pilsner Fest in October.
czechtourism.com/n/beer-tourism-september

New Zealand's Beer Tourist
Festivals, breweries, tours, and can't-miss bars.
beertourist.co.nz

NOTABLE FESTIVALS

Great American Beer Festival
Denver, Colorado
This craft beer festival is the biggest in the U.S.—in 2015 there were 750 breweries and 3,500 beers! You can even taste various hops, malts, yeasts, and water to understand how they come together to make beer.
greatamericanbeerfestival.com

Philly Craft Beer Festival
Philadelphia, Pennsylvania
Forbes named it one of the top ten beer festivals in the

U.S., and the profits go to a local children's charity.
phillycraftbeerfest.com

Great Taste of the Midwest
Madison, Wisconsin

One of the premiere Midwest beer festivals, on the shore of Lake Manona, this nonprofit event keeps it small and so sells out fast.
greattaste.org

Oregon Brewers Festival
Portland, Oregon

Entry to this five-day-long celebration of brewing held annually in late July is free. Instead, you buy a souvenir glass and pay for beers as you go.
oregonbrewfest.com

Fresh Hop Ale Festival
Yakima, Washington

This competition and beer festival takes place in the center of the U.S. hop-growing region (Yakima Valley produces about three-quarters of the nation's hops) and features West Coast beer made from wet rather than dry hops.
freshhopalefestival.com

Great Alaska Beer and Barleywine Festival
Anchorage, Alaska
This is a great pick for beer snobs with a do-gooder
streak: proceeds go to the American Diabetes Association. Only downside: it takes place in January,
when only the hardiest beer snobs will visit Alaska.
auroraproductions.net/beer-barley.html

Extreme Beer Fest
Boston and Los Angeles
Want your beer to taste like french toast or a rasp-
berry lime rickey? Want to figure out how many
IBUs you can stand? Want to try an archaeobeer?
Look no further.
beeradvocate.com/extreme/boston
beeradvocate.com/extreme/los-angeles

Festival of Wood and Barrel Aged Beer
Chicago, Illinois
The beers featured at this two-day festival are sour,
wild, sweet, and boozy. Think: braggot aged in aqua-
vit barrels, or kriek aged in cabernet barrels.
fobab.com

Qingdao International Beer Festival
Qingdao, China
This four-week (!) festival bills itself as the Asian

Oktoberfest. And if cultural fusion is not interesting enough for you, there are robots that sell beer and help with security.
qdbeerfest.com

Bruges Bier Festival
Brussels, Belgium
With more than 400 beers, meads, and ales to try, this is one of Belgium's largest beer festivals. Bring your map: the event layout mimics the geography of the city, with breweries organized geographically by street.
brugsbierfestival.be/en/home-230.html

Oktoberfest
Munich, Germany
Dating back to the Middle Ages, Munich's annual autumn festival runs for more than two weeks and features only beer conforming to the *Reinheitsgebot* that has been brewed in Munich proper, plus parades, amusement rides, and lots of traditional German fare.
oktoberfest.de/en

Mondial de la Bière
Montréal, Québec, Canada
Canada's largest festival features more than 400 beers, plus a selection of meads and ciders for tasting, as well as guided tasting tours, pairings workshops (beer and chocolate, anyone?), and offbeat offerings such as "beer yoga" sessions.
festivalmondialbiere.qc.ca/en

Blumenau Oktoberfest
Blumenau, Brazil
This festival hosted in the Brazilian city settled by Germans in 1850 marries local *cervejas* with traditional German fare.
oktoberfest-brazil.com

LIMITED RELEASES TO LOOK OUT FOR

This is hardly an exhaustive list! But here are some beer snob favorites.

Pliny the Younger
Triple IPA
Russian Brewing Company, Santa Rosa, CA

Angel of Darkness
Barrel-aged sour beer flavored with boysenberries,

blackberries, cherries, and raspberries
Wicked Weed Brewing, Asheville, NC

Focal Banger
IPA
The Alchemist, Waterbury, VT

Sexual Chocolate
Cocoa-infused imperial stout
Foothills Brewing, Winston-Salem, NC

Parabola
Imperial stout aged in expensive bourbon barrels
Firestone Walker Brewery, Paso Robles, CA

Dark Lord
Imperial stout with coffee and vanilla
3 Floyds Brewing Company, Munster, IN

Darkness
Russian imperial stout
Surly Brewing Company, Minneapolis, MN

Company Dinner
Hoppy double IPA
Maine Beer Company, Freeport, ME

Milkshake IPA
IPA brewed with oats and fruit pectin
Tired Hands Brewing Company, Ardmore, PA

EDUCATION

All the places and scholars that will teach you beer.

American Brewers Guild
abgbrew.com

Beer Judge Certification Program
bjcp.org

Beer schools
craftbeer.com/beer/beer-schools

The Beer Scholar
thebeerscholar.org

Cicerone training
cicerone.org

HOME BREWING

If you're ready to DIY, here's where to start.

American Homebrewer's Association
Includes a registry of clubs, articles, recipes, a guide to local home-brewing laws, and a search tool for home brew shops.
homebrewersassociation.org

Brew Your Own magazine
byo.com/resources

Homebrew Stack Exchange
homebrew.stackexchange.com

Homebrew Talk
homebrewtalk.com

Hops Growers of America
usahops.org

ACKNOWLEDGMENTS

Thanks to Blair Thornburgh for her expert editorial help. Thanks to Tiffany Hill, most worthy friend and colleague. Thanks to Abbi Holt and Eric McCracken for doing the hard work of helping me complete research in the field. Thanks also to Nels Nelson, Eliza Waters, Paul Gentile, and S. for advice, help, and conversations. And of course thanks to Michael Gerhard Martin for his love, support, and chile verde with lager. If you had tasted it, you would have married him, too.